SUMMARY OF

FOOD

What the Heck Should I Eat?

By Mark Hyman

Proudly Brought To You By
OneHour Reads

Disclaimer

This book is a summary and meant to be a great companionship to the original book or to simply help you get the gist of the original book. If you're looking for the original book, kindly go to Amazon website, and search for the keyword Food: What the Heck Should I Eat? By Mark Hyman.

Table of Contents

EXECUTIVE SUMMARY

There is enough confusion already about food, which ones to eat, which ones not to eat, and what not. This book, **"FOOD: What the heck should I eat"** is however not another addition to the confusing pile. Rather, Mark Hyman, with this book, aims to erase all the harmful myths we've been sold about food and replace them with the right ones.

He advocates for the consumption of natural, whole foods which he believes is the answer to pretty much everything that ails our world. Much of what we eat today is processed, and as such, is not really food in its wholeness.

In part II of the book, Hyman examines the different food groups, analyzing their scientific components, debunking myths, and providing truths about them. He makes a distinction between the healthy variants which we should eat, and the unhealthy that are to be avoided.

In parts III and IV, he explains how we can put our knowledge on the food groups to optimum use and proposes a 10-day Detox and an ideal Pegan diet.

The entire book seems premised on the departure from a processed-food culture to an adoption of natural, wholesome foods as our only choice.

Hyman provides safe, healthy food options that are not just good for us, but that also encourage sustainable environment and that are produced with best practices.

PART I

ENDING FOOD CONFUSION, FEAR, AND INSECURITY

Key Takeaways:

- *Food is a fundamental part of everything in our world*
- *The capitalistic food industry takes advantage of our ignorance on what to eat and how to prepare them, providing us with 'easier' alternatives that damage our health*
- *Food heals*
- *We must make conscious effort to know about our foods.*

The miracle of food exists all around us. That miracle refers to real food that is grown naturally in the ground, and not the overly-processed, unnatural junk that fills our store shelves. The former strengthens, restores, and enriches our lives while the latter is the root cause of most sicknesses and deaths, and pretty much everything else wrong with the world. Fortunately, the ball is in our court. We can decide which path to tread.

This book addresses and rectifies all the food myths we have grown to religiously follow. The sad part is that, while we're working with these myths, believing them to be truth, they have actually been responsible for the rise in obesity and protracted illnesses that continue to plague our nation. We forget that food can be linked to not just weight loss or gain, but is also at the foundation of our mental, psychological, emotional, and spiritual health. If more of us knew this, health insurance would not be largest weight on the American budget. Most of it is spent treating diseases that could have been avoided by eating the right food, the right way.

Food is the single most effective medicine in the whole of human history. Many do not know the numerous effects food has on the body's biological processes; the immense changes that the right food can bring about in the body, and ultimately, the entire being. Unfortunately, the science of food is hardly incorporated in the medical school syllabus so most Doctors are not trained in it. Using food as the main drug is part of a treatment approach that does not treat disease symptoms in isolation, but addresses the root cause.

Real food is becoming increasingly scarce. Our diets today consist mostly of what one might call semi-foods; industrially manufactured and containing dangerous substances like Monosodium Glutamate (MSG), High-fructose corn syrup, Trans-fats, preservatives, antibiotics, synthetic sweeteners and coloring, pesticides, and many more. Sadly for us, the food industry has succeeded in convincing most of us that we don't have to do the cooking. They'll do it for us instead, and we'll just have it easy. They carry out test studies to discover new ways of getting us hooked to their 'food products', like sugar. As such- and also with the help of government policies- they have succeeded in controlling what we eat, and ultimately, how healthy we live.

The damaging effects of the activities of the food industry can be seen in the situation of a real-life American family in South Carolina. Of the five people in the family, three were obese- father, mother, and a teenage son. The father's condition was more complicated with the fact that he had Type 2 diabetes and kidney failure. Worse still, he had to lose forty pounds before he could be eligible for a transplant, but their food & lifestyle made that pretty difficult. They lived on food stamps, also known as SNAP (Supplemental Nutrition Assistance Program), ate factory-processed foods with no fresh vegetables, dined at fast-food restaurants, and did little to no cooking. They were in a prison of ill-health and their lifestyle, the things they ate, only served to keep them longer in bondage. The only way to break out was by introducing the right type of food. So, with guidance, they learnt to cook wholesome meals, with healthy, natural ingredients- fresh vegetables and not the canned variety; salad dressing made from scratch with whole foods; the whole nine yards. After a period of nine months living this new, nutritious life, the whole family had lost considerable amount of weight, and the father had gotten a new kidney.

The popular perception is that eating healthy costs more money and takes a lot of time, but really, it's all a matter of priority. If we save money and time by eating a lot of junk, we pay for it later when we become addicted to unhealthy foods and start nursing chronic diseases. Truth is, most of us do not just know how to buy and prepare good meals. We don't even know where to start from in the kitchen so we'd rather stick to the familiar pre-cooked, overly processed, man-made stuff. We continue to fall prey to the marketing gimmicks of the notorious food industry that is mostly out to get more for less. We need to get back to cooking; equip ourselves with knowledge on the right foods, how to prepare, and how to eat them.

There are a number of reasons for the prevailing confusion when it comes to food. For one, studies or experiments on human nutrition are never accurate. This is attributed to the fact that humans themselves cannot be controlled and observed for a long period of time as with other animals. The most one can do is draw conclusions from basic scientific knowledge, concluded experiments, and apply them using our innate sense of what is good and what is not. The inaccuracy of these studies is what has resulted in the conflicting reports about what to eat and what not to eat. For instance, the American Heart Association (AHA) ruled coconut oil as unhealthy even though there are no studies proving that coconut oil is unhealthy. Coconut oil contains saturated fats which myths say causes heart diseases, but so far, no study has proved such. As a matter of fact, breast milk, which is considered highly essential for babies' growth and development, contains 25% saturated fat.

Let's also not forget that most of these researches are carried out by conducting surveys on humans, who have been found to tweak the information they provide depending on how good it makes them look.

Another major issue is the *"He who pays the piper dictates the tune"* dilemma. Nutritional studies are often sponsored by the big names in the food industry, and more often than not, the results are tilted in their favor. For instance, the AHA's study that turned out to say coconut oil is dangerous because it has saturated fats was funded by a number of food companies who had replaced saturated fats with vegetable oils in their production. These companies also pay a lot of money to the AHA for using its heart-friendly mark of approval on their products.

Biased scientists are another factor. They refuse to accept any study findings that do not align with their previously held nutritional models.

Finally, the absence of an organized and all-inclusive food policy is doing a lot of harm. The highly politicized nature of our food industry has helped to promote the consumption of unhealthy food-like substances, contributing largely to the increase in protracted diseases. The bigwigs of the food industry keep doing all they can to maximize their profits, and the government is almost no better; sweetened beverages are one of the readily available options for the over 40 million people living on food stamps. The inadequacy of our food policies have adverse effects:

- One in every two Americans suffers from life-threatening diseases linked to food and lifestyle, and resulting in an emergency in the health care sector.

- The financial implications of the above situation on the federal budget- Medicare and Medicaid.
- Food-related diseases in children leads to a continuous decline in achievements.
- An unhealthy military increases insecurity
- Climate change and Environmental decline
- Eating harmful foods affect our psychological wellbeing and behavior, which can lead to an increase in violent acts and poverty rates.

Until there is a cohesive national food, health and wellbeing policy that ties all the necessary parts together, food injustice will keep winning.

Ever heard of *Nutritionism*? It refers to the breaking down of dietary elements into their distinct part. It is a contributory factor to our food dilemma in that, it takes away our focus from the whole food and puts it on the individual components. That way, the food industry can capitalize on our narrow vision. Foods contain more than one ingredients working together in our bodies, but when we're obsessed with a particular ingredient, the big food industry players only have to tweak their marketing to suit whatever trend is holding sway.

Despite the confusion however, we all know- to a large extent- the right foods. We know we should be eating whole foods free from chemicals and industrial processing. The time has come for us to exercise our power of choice the right way. We can say no to the 'help' from food companies offering to relieve us of the stress of making our own foods while damaging our bodies. We will not just be choosing healthier bodies for ourselves, we'd also be choosing a healthier society and a healthier planet. Thousands of patients with life-threatening illnesses have had their health restored by incorporating a healthy food lifestyle into their treatment.

It is time to retrace our steps; go back to the days when humans ate real, fresh, locally-grown, and wholesome foods.

PART II
WHAT THE HECK SHOULD I EAT?

Enough with all the confusion: today, eat whole eggs; tomorrow, oh no, only egg whites are good for your health. Here's what you need to know about the major food categories.

MEAT
Key Takeaways:

- *The argument that meat is dangerous is highly inaccurate*
- *Meat is an essential part of our diet that provides protein such as we can get from no other substitute*
- *The right kind of meat can prevent heart disease and type 2 diabetes*
- *Grass-fed, locally produced meat is the best kind*
- *Offals pack even greater nutrients; cooking meat at high temperatures is detrimental to our health*

There has been a lot of buzz surrounding Meat- whether we should eat it or not. In recent times, most of the buzz has been in favor of the latter, so it's no fault of yours if you think meat is evil. But on what side should we actually be? For or against meat. Consider the fact that meat as food goes way back to the time of our ancestors who generally lived healthier lives than we do. Our ancestors ate meat combined with plants (veggies) and it would appear they knew that a Pegan (Paleo + VEGan) diet was the way to go. Recent studies also show that modern-day folks who eat and live much like our Paleolithic ancestors are generally healthier. So how can meat be the cause of obesity, cancer, and heart disease, as some groups claim? To some extent, this is because most of the meat we eat today in America are raised on factory farms and reared in unhygienic, harsh conditions that damage the environment and eventually make them poisonous to our bodies. But there is nothing scientifically wrong with eating the right meat reared in the right conditions- organic, grass-fed, and environment-friendly.

For one, meat contains an amount of protein that cannot be fund in any of the other meat substitutes (eggs, tuna, peanut butter, lentils, etc.) and we need it more to sustain our muscle mass as we grow. Although meat raised in the wrong conditions or cooked wrongly is harmful to our health, meat itself is not the demon it has generally been painted to be by the nutrition experts.

Basically, meat became the bad guy when it was discovered that saturated fat increased cholesterol in the body, which was widely regarded as the cause for the heart disease scourge in the country. It was tagged the Lipid Theory: reduce heart disease by cutting off cholesterol. But it was too narrow a view. One, because heart disease is influenced by so much more than cholesterol- blood sugar, inflammation, etc. Two, not all forms of cholesterol is bad for the body. Some forms actually help to prevent heart disease and saturated fat is also responsible for producing those. But unfortunately, the Lipid Theory myth still holds sway; it is adopted by the American Heart Association and reflected in the United States Dietary Guidelines.

Proponents of this school of thought refuse to accept evidence from more comprehensive studies that show no causal relationship between saturated fat and heart disease.

Although we shouldn't overdo our meat consumption- too much of anything is bad, anyway- it is not the killer we've been told it is. There are ongoing studies on how much of saturated fat is really healthy, but there's no need to banish meat completely from our plates.

If there's anything you should know about meat, it's these:

- Meat contains essential vitamins and minerals as cannot be found in plant substitutes. These essentials are more necessary as we age to prevent things like muscle loss, dementia, cancer, increased levels of stress hormones, and yes, heart disease.
- Bacon and any other processed meat, as long as it is locally made and organically produced does not cause cancer.
- Inevitably, we feed on whatever our meat has been fed on. This is why warnings about meat are valid; most factory farm animals are fed an assortment of waste products, hormones, and antibiotics that make them fat quickly.
- Animals fed on grass produce the healthiest and most nutritious meat.
- Conjugated Linoleic Acid (CLA), a powerful antioxidant that greatly reduces the risk of Type 2

diabetes and heart disease, can be found in the largest quantities in meat and dairy fed on grass.

- Organically produced, grass-fed meat costs almost double the price of those fed with waste and antibiotics, but that's a small price to pay for our well-being. Besides, most families are eating way more meat than they actually need.
- Offal, especially the Liver, are some of the greatest sources of animal nutrients you'll ever find, even more than beef meat.
- Cooking meat at high temperatures- frying, grilling, smoking- is dangerous to human health. Try roasting, stewing, or baking.

Studies finding meat eaters to be likely to die sooner than vegetarians often miss the fact that generally, meat eaters tend to have unhealthier lifestyle habits than those who abstain for health reasons. So, in most cases, it is those other unhealthy habits, like smoking and drinking, which contribute to the overall research findings.

Both factory-farmed and grass-fed livestock consume a lot of energy, with the former consuming way more and causing immense damage to the environment. However, the practice of regenerative farming is a solution that not only benefits us as consumers, but also the environment and even the animals.

If you're going to eat meat, take note of the following:

- Buy meat certified with these labels:
    - Certified Humane

- Global Animal Partnership
- Animal Welfare Approved
- Food Alliance Certified

- Your first choice should be Grass-fed meat. Look out for the American Grassfed Association (AGA) certification.
- Your next best choice is organic. Look out for the USDA organic certification.
- You don't need meat in large quantities. Ideally, protein should only constitute one-quarter of your plate. The rest should be vegetables.
- Eat as little processed meats as possible, and even when you do, make sure it's locally produced and free from harmful chemicals. You'll also want to stay away hotdogs that are not made wholly from pork or beef.
- Don't eat overdone meat or meats cooked at high temperatures. If you're going to cook or grill at a high temperature, at least marinate first with natural spices like rosemary, turmeric, chili, paprika, etc.

POULTRY AND EGGS
Key Takeaways:

- *Chicken meat has medicinal properties*
- *The yolk is not bad. In fact, it contains more nutrients than egg whites*
- *Pasture-raised poultry, and their eggs, are the best*

Chickens became popular in the American diet when red meat was condemned as the cause of heart disease. White meat- chicken- was what the dietary guidelines told us was a healthier substitute, so the demand skyrocketed. But as is likely to happen in such excessive demand situation, the need to create a larger supply was born, resulting in industrial rearing and a reduction in nutritional quality of our chickens- quantity over quality. The dwindling nutritional quality of chickens also led to a reduction in the quality of their products- Eggs. The fear of cholesterol also led to the nutrition experts and guidelines telling us to avoid the egg yolk and only eat egg whites. This could not have been further from the truth.

The traditional poultry comes packed with nutrients- Protein, Choline, B vitamins, Sulfur, Phosphorus, Selenium, and Iron. It also contains infection-fighting properties that makes it quite medicinal; chicken soup, remember?

But not today's industrially produced, factory farmed poultry that are fed a bunch of unsavory stuff, caged in confined enclosures, and pumped full with antibiotics to make them unnaturally fat. These are far from the locally grown poultry and cannot compete in terms of nutritional value. If you care about your health and wellbeing, you will have to go the extra mile- in terms of money and effort- to get locally grown, pasture-raised, wholesome poultry.

It has been established that heart disease and obesity are not caused by calories or fat, but by peculiar forms of each. Although chicken delivers less nutrients than beef, it still qualifies as one of the finest sources of animal-based nutrients. So the nutritional professionals of long ago were not wrong to make it the ideal breakfast. Where they missed it is in touting chicken as a healthier substitute for red meat that was condemned for containing saturated fat. Here's the thing: Chicken contains saturated fat and cholesterol too. The amount of saturated fat in chicken is less but not significantly. They also warned against consuming the egg yolk, saying it increases cholesterol levels, but subsequent studies have found no causal link between consumption of whole eggs and cholesterol levels, heart disease, or stroke. The limit provided by dietary guidelines was one egg per day, but all evidence show that those who eat more than one egg per day had a lower risk of heart disease.

A recent argument that is yet to be confirmed is that choline, present in egg yolks, can be metabolized by our bodies into TMAO, a compound that may increase one's risk of atherosclerosis. Research findings so far however seem to debunk this emerging theory but we know choline is an essential nutrient that helps our body on so many levels. In any case, most of these 'arguments' are created by antagonists of animal-based foods of all kinds. They also claim that eating poultry increases one's risk of cancers, but various comprehensive studies have proven that people who eat more poultry and fish are less likely to develop cancers.

If there's anything you should know about poultry and eggs, it's these:

- Chicken labels may carry some terms and you need to know what it means when you see them:
    - **Natural**- is basically saying nothing. There are no synthetic chickens;
    - **Fresh**- this only means the chicken was not frozen. It doesn't say though whether it was slaughtered a long time ago;
    - **Cage Free**- means nothing when it comes to the chicken we buy for meat. Only chickens reared for eggs are caged;
    - **Free Range**- means the chickens were allowed to go outside for a while, but doesn't imply that they *actually* went outside or what they were fed with;
    - **Antibiotic-free**- means they weren't fattened with antibiotics, but doesn't say what they were fed or how they were raised;
    - **Arsenic-free**- pretty much means the same as antibiotic-free. It signifies

that they were not fattened with Arsenic;

- **Hormone-free-** it's pointless. Administering hormones to poultry is illegal anyway;
- **Vegetarian-** is more or less a deceptive labeling. Chickens cannot be vegetarians;
- **Organic-** means the chickens were not fed chemical-laced grains or pumped with antibiotics, and they were given access to go out;
- **Certified humane-** means the chickens were raised in acceptable conditions;
- **Pastured-** this signifies chickens that were raised without any inhibitions or chemicals, free to wander wherever they liked and feed on whatever they wanted. These chickens are usually the most nutritious because chickens naturally feed on gut and insects in the dirt. They are also the most difficult- and expensive- to find.

If you don't find any of these labels, then that chicken was raised in cruel conditions on a factory farm, fed chemical-laced grains, and pumped with antibiotics/arsenics. It will be the cheapest and least nutritious chicken. Not only are they detrimental to our health, raising them also damages the environment, contributing to climate change.

New regulations were approved in 2017 by the federal Office of Management and Budget. The regulations- *Organic Livestock and Poultry Practices (OLPP)* - were meant to enforce best practices for organic farming and would have gone into effect in March 2018. Unfortunately, the Trump administration put that on hold, and it is only hoped that it would eventually be effected.

- Labels on Egg cartons can also be as deceptive as some on Poultry packs. Basically, the same explanations provided above also go for eggs, with the addition of a few:
  - **Gluten-Free**- This is just so you get the impression you're buying something healthy. There is absolutely no basis for the claim because all eggs are gluten-free;
  - **Raised on shady porches**- ignore the traditional barnyard imagery this evokes. It has a totally different meaning when it comes to poultry farming.
- It's okay to eat the yolk because that's where the bulk of nutrients reside.
- Poultry, especially those pumped with antibiotics, are very likely to harbor harmful, drug-resistant bacteria and cause food poisoning. As much as you

can, always buy organic and cook your poultry thoroughly to kill germs. Similarly, wash your eggs with warm water before cracking.

- Chicken nuggets are processed chicken that have been combined with a variety of other ingredients including chemical preservatives, and at the end of the day, they are anything but chicken.

Arsenic is fed to chickens to fatten them up, but when they are slaughtered and end up on our plates, that arsenic, studies have found, makes one more susceptible to some types of cancers, such as lung and bladder cancer.

Pasture- raised chickens are the best but they may be not as readily available as the industrial mass-produced ones in the stores. Try finding a trustworthy vendor at your local farmers' market or using some of the numerous resources available online to locate the healthy option. And yes, chickens are not the only poultry. Once in a while, you can try other options like duck and turkey.

MILK AND DAIRY
Key Takeaways:

- *Milk is bad for our health;*
- *The milk our grandparents drank is different from what we are drinking today;*
- *Milk has been linked to increased risk of cancer;*
- *The fats in milk is not the enemy;*
- *If you must, eat only grass-fed milk & dairy products*

Milk is probably one of the most misrepresented foods of all time. All the experts- government authorities, scientists & nutritionists, the food industry- lie to us about it. They tell us how much we need it for essential vitamins and how much children need it for calcium to grow strong bones. But most research findings only reveal how unnecessary it is at best, and harmful at worst. Specific findings have proven that milk actually weakens our bones. On the other hand, there are those advocating for the consumption of strictly low-fat milk; a result of the Lipid Theory mentioned earlier. This has resulted in more sweetened milks that are more likely to cause obesity. The fat in milk is not the problem. It's that the milk we drink today contains so much more unhealthy stuff, a reflection of the harmful chemicals and antibiotics fed to factory-farm cows.

Apart from the saturated and unsaturated fats contained in milk and other dairy products, zinc, calcium, riboflavin, niacin, selenium, and magnesium are also nutrients that can be found. Contrary to what most of us think, vitamins such as A, B6, B12, and D are only added. Yes, Milk is good, but its ultimate function is growth, which is why for so many people, the ability to digest it continually declines after age 2. But today's milk gotten mostly from cows raised in the worst of conditions, is not so good for our bodies. It has been found to be a foremost cause of food allergy in children. Thankfully, in recent times, the rate at which Americans consume milk and dairy is reducing.

Basically, all the goodness of milk messages we've been sold- by the USDA, in conjunction with the huge dairy sector- are false. There may be some good to be gotten from eating Yoghurt or butter or cheese (in small quantities) but definitely not milk. And lactose intolerance is definitely not the only reason why we need to stay away from milk.

Keep in mind the following about milk and dairy products:

- The prominent position of milk and dairy products in the US Dietary guidelines are the result of years of lobbying and government funding by the giant dairy industry. Similarly, the industry regularly sponsors researches, and a comparison between the sponsored and unsponsored researches reveal that the former often found health benefits linked to the consumption of milk than the latter.
- Milk does not build stronger bones.
- Healthier sources of calcium include Sardines, Mustard greens, Spinach, roasted dry Almonds, Sesame seeds, Turnip greens, Tofu, etc.
- The highly industrialized milk and dairy industry produces milk filled with hormones that are harmful

to human health, and these hormones have been found to increase one's risk of cancer.

- Some types of saturated fat have been found to prevent heart disease and Type 2 Diabetes. Low-fat or skimmed milk on the other hand, increases one's chances of obesity.
- Grass-fed butter free from harmful chemicals, is good for the body. Just don't eat it with carbs or sugar. Don't overdo it either.
- Grass-fed dairy products is the ideal. They come packed with a healthy ratio of omega-6: omega-3s fats.
- Goats' milk is healthier than the milk of modern, factory-farm cows.

There's a lot of controversy over the consumption of raw milk. It is even illegal to buy or sell it in some states. The argument against is the fact that there has been a high rate of sicknesses and deaths from the consumption of raw milk. On the other hand, those in favor cite the fact that raw milk is more easily digested than the ones gotten from conventional cows because the former comes from grass-fed cows. It is also considered to be more beneficial to our wellbeing. But the bottom-line still remains that we should not even be drinking milk. We can get the same nutrients in it from other great food sources.

Not only are milk and dairy bad for us, they are not so great for the environment either.

So if you really must take milk and dairy, eat only grass-fed, whole milk and dairy products. Goats' and sheep' milk are also better alternatives. Stay away from anything low-fat or skimmed, processed, or containing chemical additives and preservatives.

FISH AND SEAFOOD
Key Takeaways:

- *Fish provide us with much needed omega-3 fats*
- *Wild-caught fish is the best and industrially reared fish are the least nutritious*
- *Small fish are generally more nutritious and less toxic than big fish*
- *We should eat fish at least three times weekly*

It is no news that fish are highly nutritional; even developing fetuses benefit from their nutrients. They contain Omega-3 fats which have been found useful in the prevention of conditions like inflammation, type 2 diabetes, depression, and autoimmune diseases. This has led to an increased demand for fish which our waters are unable to satisfy. Hence, fish farming in factories continue to multiply on a large scale. The resulting problem is similar to every other animal-based food's: a tilt towards quantity over quality. Drug-resistant antibiotics are fed to factory-farm fishes that are more susceptible to infections in their often overcrowded spaces. Fish farmers are also finding it more difficult to give the fish quality feeds and are giving them substances mixed with chemicals, which eventually tell on human wellbeing. Sadly, as much as it is advisable to eat fish caught in their natural habitat, that itself poses great risks nowadays. For years, industries have dumped their waste in our waters, releasing harmful chemicals- like Mercury- which are absorbed by the fish, and eventually, human consumers of fish. The trick is to know how to eat the right kind of fish without falling prey to all the risks lurking around.

Fish, and seafood generally, are not only great sources of protein. They also deliver a bouquet of nutrients such as of iodine, selenium, and vitamins. Fish are more unique in that they exclusively provide us with two Omega-3 fatty acids, DHA and EPA, which are pivotal in the prevention of heart-related diseases, autoimmune diseases, diabetes, arthritis, etc. Experts have gone as far as suggesting that Omega-3 fats be a part of every human's diet. Vegetarians argue that there are plants which can produce DHA and EPA, but the levels they produce are highly inadequate for us. One of the major causes of fatal illnesses today is chronic inflammation as a result of too little omega-3 fats and too much omega-6 fats in our diets.

There has always been agreement on how healthy and nutritious fish is for us, but unfortunately, many of us eat it in the wrong forms- deep-fried fish, fish and chips, etc. Children and pregnant women are also directed to eat less of fish with mercury, such as Tuna.

For a long time however, the dietary guidelines, with their misplaced fear of saturated fats, advised against consumption of fish and seafood with high levels of cholesterol. Now however, we know that the level of cholesterol contained in fish has no impact on the level of cholesterol in our bodies. So, we can eat shrimps without thinking it would increase our risk of heart-related diseases. On another note, the dietary guidelines also failed to inform us that not all fish contain omega-3 fats in the same quantities.

You should keep these bits of information about fish in mind:

- Small fish contain the best nutrients. The bigger fish are usually at the top of the water so they absorb more waste such as mercury, and are more likely to be toxic than small fish. Sardines, herring, mackerel, anchovies, and salmon are great sources of omega-3 fats. On the other hand, Tilapia, crab, cod and lobster are some of the seafood with low omega-3 fats.
- Years of research by experts have found DHA and EPA to be effective in combating depression and other mental health conditions like suicide, psychosis, and ADHD in children. Little wonder fish is called brain food.
- Low-mercury fish works wonders for fetuses but a study has shown that pregnant women are not eating enough. Low-mercury fish like sardines and herrings should be combined with fish oil supplements and taken regularly during pregnancy.
- Because of the high demand for fish, there are a lot of fakes out there. Misleading labels are not a rarity with fish nowadays, so it would be best if you can buy you wild, safe fish from vendors you trust.

- You might want to stay off canned tuna. Although it is convenient, it comes with less nutrients and easily accessible mercury (especially for kids). Other canned fish that are caught from the sea and preferably preserved in olive oil are okay.
- Even though sushi seems like a healthy choice of fish, it really isn't. It passes more mercury on to the consumer, and because it is overwhelmed with unhealthy carbs and sugar during preparation, the nutritional value is highly diminished.
- The bulk of farmed fish are lacking in the right nutrients, containing more of the unhealthy omega-6 fats than the highly beneficial omega-3. Wild salmon can be pretty expensive, but the benefits to your health and entire wellbeing is worth it. Besides, factory-farming of fish is also cruel on the fish and the environment.
- As much as you might want to take advantage of all the nutrients in different kinds of fish and seafood, remember that they almost all of them are contaminated with mercury. The trick is to know which ones have higher and which have lower degrees of contamination. The following have the lowest degree of contamination:
  - Wild salmon
  - Scallops
  - Tilapia
  - Clams
  - Squid, and others.

The seafood with the highest degrees of contamination include:

- Swordfish
- Tuna
- Tilefish
- Bigeye tuna
- King mackerel
- Orange roughy, and others.

There are other substances that contaminate fish, especially those reared in factory-farms which have been found more likely to cause diabetes in consumers. You can cook and skin your fish to reduce your exposure to these substances.

While taking fish oil to supplement our omega-3 fats supply from fish and seafood, one must be careful to take the right one. Some fish oil supplements are gotten from factory-farmed fish that have been fed unhealthy substances and reared in nasty conditions. Expectedly, their products will be less than optimal. Krill oil is also a good alternative for fish oil supplements.

Finding good fish can be difficult amidst all the deception with labeling, but you can find a trusted fishery, or get resources online. Better still, look out for certifications from best practices establishments like Gulf Wild or the Wild Alaska Pure logo that only appears on Alaskan salmon caught in the wild.

Ideally, fish and seafood should feature in our diets not less than three times weekly.

VEGETABLES
Key Takeaways:

- *Vegetables contain phytonutrients that wards off diseases*
- *Locally grown vegetables are best because they do not contain pesticides*
- *Starchy vegetables such as potatoes are to be limited*
- *Unpopular vegetables are usually the most nutritious*

Growing up, we all heard how important it was to eat our vegetables. It was- and still is- one of the most serious topics of discussion between an unwilling child and the parent. But what exactly is the big deal about vegetables? It's weird because we know that most of the nutrients our body needs (in their ideal quantities) are gotten from animal-based foods. Vegetables provide little of the essential fats and amino acids that we require to function. They contain the right kind of carbs, but carbs are not essential. Basically, we can do without them. So why the hype over veggies? It is because they contain what we call phytonutrients, peculiar compounds that specialize in combating diseases. They also contain vitamins and minerals.

Vegetables may not be packed full as animal-based foods, but they do have their place. They were definitely one of the reasons our ancestors lived longer than us. Our forefathers' diets consisted largely of vegetables, our only source of Fiber. Fiber facilitates the circulation of digested food throughout the body. None of the meat or poultry or egg we eat would be able to deliver their benefits to our body without the presence of fiber, which is why it has been found to prevent heart-related diseases and cancer. It also helps with weight loss. And then of course, there are the phytonutrients, acting as protectors for our bodies. Unfortunately, for the longest time, we have been misinformed about vegetables. Vegetables that do not contain starch, like spinach and kale, are much more advisable. They should also form a large three-quarter of every meal, with meat or any other animal-based protein only making up a quarter. Americans have come to prefer the least nutritious- some, harmful- vegetables like iceberg lettuce, potatoes, and tomatoes. The hero veggies like Kale, radishes, and collard greens are not so highly favored by majority. When it comes to vegetables, the most nutritious ones are the bitter-tasting, dark-looking ones that are not immediately appealing to the eye; the ones that have not been affected by high demand and tainted by genetic variations.

The following are some important information about veggies:

- Their different colors signify the different phytonutrients they carry. You'll do well to eat as many colors you can find. For instance,
    - The redness of bell peppers and tomatoes indicate the presence of Lycopene which helps to prevent heart-related diseases and cancer.

- The green color of broccoli and kale is as a result of various phytochemicals that aid detoxification and hinder cancer-causing agents.
- Alpha-carotene produces the orange color of carrots, and gives you a better skin and eyesight.

- The increasing use of pesticides in industrial farming puts us at risk of so many diseases. Because of this, we must buy organic as much as we can, especially with veggies such as tomatoes, hot peppers, kale, spinach, etc.
- Take note how you prepare your veggies. You don't want to wash away all the nutrients or kill them by overcooking.
- Broccolis and leafy greens are some of the healthiest vegetables because although they are carbs, they do not adversely affect your blood sugar. Unlike vegetables like corn and potatoes.
- Yes, some vegetables can cause allergic reactions for some people. Tomatoes and potatoes are some of the vegetables quite a lot of people find difficult to digest. This can lead to inflammation, insulin resistance, and eventually, an array of chronic diseases.
- Seaweed, though not popular, is one of the most nutrient-packed vegetables you can get.

- Studies have shown that fermenting vegetables makes their composites more effective. Fermented veggies are also good for gut health.

Vegetables with a lower glycemic load- kale, tomatoes, salad greens, etc. – are safer to consume in large quantities than those with higher glycemic loads- sweet corn, potatoes, etc.

Locally grown, organic vegetables are not only best for our health and wellbeing, they are also best for the environment. You can always shop at the nearest farmers' market if you can't grow your veggies.

If you're really serious about getting the best vegetables, look out for the weird, unpopular, unpleasant-tasting ones. Such veggies are usually packed full with nutrients. Better still, they are not industrially produced so they won't be filled with pesticides or other toxic chemicals that are harmful to our health.

FRUIT
Key Takeaways:

- *Fruit is not something to binge on*
- *Organic, locally-produced fruit is the best option*
- *Fruit juice and smoothies do not give you the same nutrition as eating fruits*

Fruits have often been lumped together with vegetables, and for most of us, fruits are the easier route; they're generally tastier than veggies, especially the good ones which aren't so sweet. But that 'sweetness' is what also makes fruit something we must eat with caution. Sometimes there is no different between some of our favorite fruits and candy.

Fruit in contemporary times is different from what it was when our forefathers lived. As with every other food, commercialization has influenced the production of fruits. Sweet fruits are what is readily available, and in most cases, they pack the least nutrients. Thankfully, we still have some all-natural wild fruits, such as berries, that have incredible medicinal properties. We can still benefit from their antioxidant, anti-inflammatory properties by simply getting a bag of frozen blackberries or elderberries. Let's not forget that fruits also have anti-cancer properties.

All the nutrition experts and authorities agree that fruits are highly nutritious and should be encouraged. Some of its identified benefits include vitamins, antioxidants, fiber, and general disease prevention. Unfortunately, most Americans are not taking advantage of these benefits. Why? Because we favor the wrong fruits. Studies reveal that the favored fruits of Americans are orange juice, bananas, and apple juice, all of which do not have the nutrition we need. Worse, there is a link between consumption of juices and diabetes.

What should you know about fruit?

- The sugar in fruits, known as Fructose, is also often used as artificial sweetener in most sodas and processed beverages. In its industrial, artificial form, it has been found to facilitate the breakdown of the liver and increase the chances of obesity. Fortunately, in its natural form in fruits, fructose often comes with fiber that helps to guard against the otherwise damaging sugar. The fiber is also good for your gut health. Fructose is the major reason why you don't want to binge on fruits.
- Not all fruits are healthy. Some fruits have lower glycemic loads, meaning they do not raise your blood sugar as much. Such fruits include watermelon and orange. Others, like bananas and raisins, have a high glycemic load, significantly raise your blood sugar, and should be avoided.
- Berries come packed with the most amount of antioxidants, which prevents a lot of chronic illnesses like heart-related disease and cancer.
- You're better off buying organic fruit. Conventionally produced fruits always carry remains of pesticides that are harmful to human health, and in most cases, washing the fruit does not take them all out.

- Believe it or not, frozen fruit is often healthier than fresh fruit. While fresh fruit are harvested before they ripen to avoid rots, frozen fruits are harvested ripe, filled with their complete nutrients, and frozen immediately, which locks in the nutrients.
- Fruit juice and smoothies do not deliver the same nutrition as eating organic, whole fruits. Worse still, with commercially produced juices and smoothies, there's the possibility that it's not all natural anymore.

The transportation of fruit from their producers to the shelves has not had the best impacts on the environment. So also, the increasing demand for some fruits have resulted in loss of greenery beneficial to our climate. These effects can be combated by buying organic or growing your own fruits locally.

A few fruits contain fats; the good kind. Avocado, olives, and coconuts contain healthy fats that help prevent cancer and heart-related disease, and boost the functioning of the brain.

So basically, you should eat fruits like blackberries, blueberries, plum, grapefruit, papayas, and even the strange-sounding ones, like snake fruit. They are hardly produced on a large commercial scale so there are lesser chances that they've been tainted with pesticides. Do your best to stay away from sugary fruits like pineapples and bananas, and if you must eat them, take reduced quantities.

More than anything however, remember, organic is the way to go.

FATS AND OILS
Key Takeaways:

- *Fats are not the enemy*
- *Our bodies benefit more from fats and oils than from carbs*
- *The best kinds of fats and oils are the whole, unrefined ones found in animals and plants*
- *High-fat diets actually increase weight loss*

This is one of the most misrepresented food groups known to man. We were told to avoid Fats and oils and to eat only sparingly if we had to. One of the misconception was that it makes us fat, and the other, graver claim was that it causes heart disease. For the longest time, the dietary guidelines, without any scientific proof, warned us not to eat fats and oils because they got the facts wrong. The first was the wrong assumption that the fats we eat become the fats in our bodies. The second was that since carbs had lesser calories than fats, the latter induces weight gain. But scientific studies have revealed that fats increase our body metabolism, which in turn helps us to lose weight. The third untruth was that saturated fats and cholesterols are responsible for heart disease. The result was an increase in consumption of carbs and the substitution of animal fats with trans fats- both highly healthy choices. Extensive scientific studies have debunked the unfavorable myths about fats and oils, but not everyone has accepted the truth. And maybe the fact that understanding fats can be sometimes difficult- *Which is good? Which is bad? –* also adds to the propagation of these myths.

Now, we've all been taught that carbohydrates give us energy; fuel on which our body runs. But most of us likely do not know that fats are also fuel burned by our bodies, and even better than carbs because they don't increase our blood sugar as carbs do. They speed up our metabolism, helping us burn way more calories and lose weight. There's nothing wrong with the fats that come from our traditional, natural, whole plant and animal foods; it's the commercially processed stuff we should worry about. Natural fats facilitate immune cells and hormone production, healthy cell membranes, and the regulation of inflammation and metabolism.

The experts and authorities, for a very long time, got it wrong on this one. They told us to stay away from foods containing fat. They agree that we all need omega-3 fats but still say we should limit our consumption of saturated fats. Tough! These misleading directions led to a decrease in Americans' consumption of fat and an increase in carbs and sugars. The result? An increase in obesity and diabetes rates. The highly demonized saturated fats continue to be vindicated by studies which repeatedly find no links between it and heart disease. A lot of research is being done however, to enhance our understanding of the different kinds of saturated fats.

You should know these about fats and oils:

- MUFA (Monounsaturated fatty acids) in its natural form is very healthy for us. They serve as prevention against heart-related diseases and reduce the bad kind of cholesterol. You can find them in foods like avocado, chicken fat, olive oil, and butter. When they are processed and refined however, MUFAs can become very toxic.

- Our bodies need polyunsaturated fats, precisely omega-3 fats and omega-6 fats. Omega-3 fats are the better of the two because they are anti-inflammatory and have been proven effective in combating mental health problems like Alzheimer's disease, suicide, depression, etc. Omega-3 fats are best found in meat from grass-fed animals, fatty wild fish and seafood, walnuts, etc. best sources of omega-6 fats include whole grains, nuts and beans.

- The lie that saturated fats are harmful to our bodies has been debunked by years and years of scientific studies- over and over again. Our bodies need saturated fats. In fact, it is healthier to cook with saturated fats like coconut oil and butter because they do not turn toxic when exposed to heat.

- Consuming Trans fats- or more accurately, hydrogenated vegetable or soybean oil- increases the chances of obesity, diabetes, heart-related disease, and even cancer. Look out for the word "hydrogenated" on ingredient lists because not all "zero trans fats" really mean "ZERO trans fats"

- Eat your veggies with natural, whole fats. Many of the vitamins you cherish in vegetables can only be absorbed into your body with the help of fat. So no, don't avoid fat or use a low-fat dressing.

- Olive oil is unarguably one of the healthiest oils, but it can turn unhealthy with just a little heat applied so it is best used raw. Furthermore, the high demand for it has resulted in a lot of fakes being paraded as the real thing.
- Coconut oil has been condemned by the American Heart Association (AHA), but considering that this organization is highly influenced by the big-time cereal makers who sell 'low fat, high-sugar' products, we can't be too surprised. Scientific evidence and observations agree however that coconut oil is highly nutritious. It increases production of the right kind of cholesterol and generally prevents heart disease. It also produces MCT oil, a saturated fat that not only facilitates weight loss but also boosts cerebral functioning.
- Keto diets are healthy because they stimulate our bodies to burn fats instead of carbs. The result is a cleaner body and a sharper brain.

The production of oils can be detrimental to the environment. Oils like olive oil and coconut oil have resulted in deforestation practices that continue to enhance climate change and promote dehumanization of workers. To combat this, we can buy organic and look out for certifications such as the CSPO labeling and Fair Trade USA.

When it comes to fats and oils, you want to eat the healthy, natural ones gotten from whole foods, such as butter from grass-fed animals, not the overly refined, processed, and toxic stuff. And remember, the best things to combine healthy fats and oils with is healthy, whole veggies, not sugar or carbs.

BEANS
Key Takeaways:

- *Beans are not as healthy as we've been led to believe*
- *Beans are environment-friendly, unlike most other foods*
- *Eat organic & avoid canned beans*
- *Soybeans is not all that fantastic*

Beans can be a pretty foregone conclusion: of course, it's healthy! Who can argue with beans? We all grew up with our parents telling us how good they are and even the dietary guidelines agree. Various studies have also found beans to be instrumental in the prevention of diseases and overall optimal performance of our bodies. So, do we still need any more?

Beans are plant seeds that carry a high concentration of nutrients. Their ability to take in nitrogen needed for growth from the atmosphere also makes them high protein carriers. And it also means they can thrive in the poorest soil conditions, needing very little concentrations of fertilizer.

Yes, beans come packed with their fair share of nutrients- protein, fiber, zinc, potassium, vitamins etc. Remember that fiber is good for gut health. Planting beans also has less adverse effects on the environment so they're environment-friendly. Lastly, some studies have suggested that consumption of beans might have an effect on lesser heart disease and death risks.

But beans also come packed with starchy carbs that increase our blood sugar. However, the carbs contained in beans are significantly different from those carried in grains and if you're going to eat carbs at all, eat the one in beans. But they are a no-go for anyone with diabetes of any kind. Beans also contain Lectins and Phytates, which inhibit our access to vital nutrients, and can very well lead to inflammation and blood clotting. Unfortunately, cooking in most cases only strengthen these substances, causing even greater damage to our bodies. Fermentation is a much more effective alternative.

We know beans contains protein, but many of us are not aware that its protein is of little to no nutritional value to our bodies. The protein we find in animals are more valuable to us than beans. Worse still, beans can aid gut malfunctioning. It's the reason why some people get gas and inflammation after eating beans. Beans have their healthy features, but they also have their bad sides, so you may want to hold off on bingeing on this supposed 'health food'.

It is not completely established how everyone reacts to beans, but we do know that it is best avoided by people suffering from diabetes or autoimmune disease. You need to know that:

- If you're looking for the amount of protein necessary for optimum performance of your body, beans is not it. It cannot even provide the required protein levels for muscle formation, something we need more as we grow older.

- The carbs in beans are known as resistant starch. Basically, they do not have the same damaging effects that grain starch has on our bodies. As a matter of fact, they act more like fiber than starch and prevent cancer. Letting cooked beans cool before eating them works to increase their resistant starch and overall nutritional value.

- Beans can worsen stomach troubles, so if you have irritable bowel syndrome or reflux, your gut will not be helped by beans consumption.

- Lectins and Phytates found in beans can result in leaky gut, diabetes, depression, etc.

- Canned beans are not a healthy option because not only do they contain harmful amounts of sodium, their cans may also contain the dangerous chemical, BPA that has been shown to increase risks of sexual dysfunction in males, diabetes, obesity, etc.

- Green peas and Green beans have significantly lesser amounts of starch than most beans, so they are healthy choices.

- Many have no idea that peanuts are beans too. They carry the same bouquet of nutrients but they also come with omega-6 fats. For this reason, they should only be consumed moderately. Peanut oil and peanut butter should also be avoided because asides the omega-6 fats, they are highly processed and refined with a bunch of toxic chemical additives that are bad news to our bodies.

- Soybeans does not completely live up to its 'health food' hype. If you must eat it, eat only organic and you don't need it in large quantities. Tempeh and Tofu are very healthy variants if you're looking to eat some soybeans.
- Soybean oil, soymilk, and virtually every soy product is dangerous for human health. Soybean oil is a major source of omega-6 fats, and because it is what fast foods and restaurants use, we have been consuming it for a long time; we still do. Processed soy protein, which produces all these soy products, has been found to cause cancer.

Beans are a recent agricultural discovery, unlike meat and vegetables that our cavemen ancestors during their time. Because of this, some groups advocate that it should be excluded from human diet. Subsequent evidence has however shown that the early men and women ate wild peas and beans. Paleo societies today still eat beans too, even though they're mostly the uncommon types.

Beans are not bad, but unlike the generalized myths, you may want to restrict yourself to eating it only once or twice weekly. You'll also do well to soak it overnight before cooking.

Organic varieties like Tofu are healthy choices. Beans containing low starch like peas are also good. Garbanzo beans, asparagus beans, snow peas, etc are all examples of beans you can eat. On the other hand, you'll want to stay away from foods like peanuts, baked beans, and anything in a can.

GRAINS
Key Takeaways:

- *We do not need grains to be healthy*
- *Unusual grains are the best*
- *Oatmeal is not so healthy*
- *Consumption of grains promote obesity and diabetes*

There is nothing Americans consume in larger quantities than grains. It is everywhere. From our breakfast oatmeal and cereals, to breads and baked desserts, pizza, you name it! Even the government subsidizes grain-based crops such as sorghum, corn, rice, and wheat, from which we make flour. That's not all, the bulk of our animal foods are fed subsidized grains which we eventually ingest when they reach our plates. Unfortunately, all this is too much starch that has been weakening and destroying human bodies for years.

Grains were never a part of our cavemen and women ancestors' diets. Simply put, grains are the seeds of certain grass, and when we discovered them about a thousand decades ago, they seemed like a miracle discovery. But it has been revealed that our physical skeletons shrunk in size as a result of our consumption of grains. That doesn't sound good.

Grains are not without some good. They contain fiber which regulate digestion, flushes out toxins from the body, promotes wellbeing of our gut, and generally prevent disease such as cancer. Grains also contain vitamins, proteins, minerals such as potassium, and even some fats. But they also contain generous deposits of starch which increase our sugar blood and leads to complications such as diabetes and obesity.

Probably the greatest fraud committed in the history of human nutrition is the nutrition experts and government authorities telling us to cut our fats and stock up on carbs. The dietary guidelines that advised us to replace our fats with grains is responsible for the deaths of so many who followed that directive. Obesity, diabetes, dementia, heart-related diseases, and even cancer have all been linked to diets high in grains. Unfortunately, much of these erroneous statements are still believed by many. As such, these diseases will not go away unless we put an end to our widespread grain-dependence.

Let's go back to our ancestors who ate no grains and still lived longer than the average human today. We can do without grains. It may sound weir since we know grains do carry some healthy nutrients, but in reality, we can get all the nutrients found in grains from other foods- mostly veggies- that do not put us at risk of the deadly carbs.

Grains contain high concentrations of starch, and starch, at the end of the day, is just sugar is our bodies. In the real sense of eat, wheat flour deposits more sugars into our system than actual table sugar. It's worse because flour is refined grain and that process has stripped the grain of the nutrients it possesses. It is no wonder then that a high-carb diet has been linked to obesity and diabetes, and found to influence cancer and well. Using flour made from other foods like coconuts can be a healthier alternative.

Consuming Gluten activates a series of processes in our bodies that produce leaky gut syndrome and a condition called Celiac. Celiac has been found to lead to an array of chronic illnesses such as kidney diseases, cancer, psychiatric disorders, etc.

Most of the grains we eat today are genetically modified and packed full with all kinds of things- toxics, pesticides, fertilizers, etc. - that simply put, kill our bodies.

Don't feel too safe when you see grain-based products carrying 'Gluten free' tags. It only means that the gluten has been taken out and replaced with other refined, overly processed artificial additives that may actually be worse for your health.

Cereals- even the ones that claim to be healthy, sugar free, etc. – should not be your breakfast choice. Not only do they carry the dangers of refined grains, they are usually sold with deceptive labeling to mislead the consumer. They promote a sugar addiction culture that is continually increasing the rate of obesity, heart disease, and diabetes cases.

Oatmeal is still grain, no matter how 'healthy' we've come to think of it as. It increases our blood sugar and food cravings, contributing to the increased rates of obesity and diabetes. Studies have also revealed that eating oatmeal leads to not just higher levels of sugar and insulin, but also cortisol, a harmful hormone.

Corn, for the most part is healthy. Whole, natural corn provides us with much needed fiber, antioxidants, essential vitamins and minerals, etc. but if you're going to eat corn, eat only organic. Popular genetically modified corn has significantly lesser nutrients, plus, it comes with a lot of toxic baggage that your body can do without.

Rice should not be your staple food. White rice, especially has little to no nutritional value. Brown, purple, red, and black rice are less starchy and contain more fiber that your body can use. Asides that, rice is easily contaminated with pesticides and arsenic, so even if you must eat rice, reduce your consumption.

Not surprisingly, some of the healthiest grains are the uncommon ones, the ones you won't find easily in your supermarket. Quinoa is one of such grains. They contain way lesser starch and are not genetically modified or 'refined'.

Asides from these, the cultivation of grain itself is not so great on the environment. It rapidly destroys the soil, and farmers, trying to combat this side effect, introduce more fertilizers and pesticides, which equal greater poisoning for the grains and the soil. It can be pretty difficult to get healthy, wholesome, untainted grains.

If you do have to eat grains, are sure they are organic, whole, gluten-free, and whole. Folks with digestive complications, diabetes, autoimmune disease, or bloating should stay away from grains. Completely!

NUTS AND SEEDS
Key Takeaways:

- *We can eat more of nuts & seeds*
- *The fat in nuts & seeds is good for us*
- *Nuts & seeds are antioxidant-rich cancer-prevention guys*
- *1 or 2 handfuls of nuts & seeds a day is fine*
- *Only buy and eat organic*

Nuts and seeds had it rough at the time dietary guidelines demonized anything containing fats. It fell into the category of foods we were advised to eat only in the least quantity. They became one of those foods we don't just see as important. How wrong we are! Nuts are not only cool because they do not have carbs that increase our blood sugar, but they also come packed with fats, protein, fiber, and a host of other nutritional goodness.

Nuts contain fats, including the very essential omega-3 fats. The misconception for so long was that nuts make us fatter, but recent evidence have proven otherwise. Nuts promote weight loss, optimal body functioning, and prevention of diseases such as diabetes and cancer. One of the factors that strengthened our misconceptions about nuts is the way it has been prepared for years. If we're not dousing them in salt, then it's in chocolate sauce or some other highly sugary, refined, and unhealthy substance.

Countless studies have shown that nuts are as good as any drug to reduce the risks of having kidney disease, strokes and heart attacks.

Nuts come packed with the good kind of calories; the kind that does not increase our blood sugar levels as carbs do. Nuts promote weight loss, not weight gain.

Nuts are natural cancer-prevention heroes. Hazelnuts and Pecans are some of the nuts with the highest amount of antioxidants.

As absurd as it sounds, the skins of nuts are highly nutritional and should be eaten.

Seeds also provide a healthy concentration of omega-3 fats, fiber, minerals, proteins, and antioxidants. Remember to add seeds such a chia seeds and sesame seeds regularly to your diet.

Nut products such a butter, flour, and milk are alright as long as you can vouch for their wholeness and unrefined state. Besides, only eat them in moderation.

As with beans, Lectins and Phytates are present in nuts and seeds as well, and you can reduce them by soaking overnight in warm water. And yes, if you're going to eat nuts and seeds, eat organic. *That* cannot be stressed enough!

SUGAR AND SWEETENERS
Key Takeaways:

- *Sugar and sweeteners have done unquantifiable damage to human health over the years*
- *All sugar is addictive*
- *Cultivation of sugar is hurting the environment*

With the amount of damage it does to our bodies, sugar shouldn't even be considered as food. It has been linked to so many diseases- diabetes, obesity, heart disease, depression, you name it! Yet, we continue to consume sugars in unhealthy proportions. Yes, sugars are sweet, which make them instinctively appealing, and the long-touted low-fat, high-carb diet has pretty much gotten us addicted to sugar, but now we know better, and need to take conscious efforts to change our ways. Realistically, this can be pretty difficult, given that most of the sugar that finds its way into our bodies is not from our prepared foods, but from everything else we buy at the store, on the streets, the fast food outlets, and restaurants. We are daily pumped with sugar way more than our bodies can handle. Basically, the entire food industry is sugar-driven.

Among the many negatives of sugar in our bodies, the following are a few:

- Increase in blood sugar levels which can lead to diabetes
- Consumption of sugar leads to an increased risk of dementia
- It produces fatty liver that leads to liver damage

- It is linked to increased rates of cancer

And sweeteners are no better. The mere fact that they are 'artificial' is a red flag, and they also promote sugar addiction, diabetes, and obesity.

Nutrition experts and doctors generally have always warned of the dangers of sugar, but when the dietary guidelines of 1980 struck out fats and gave a thumbs-up to sugar, a scourge was unleashed. Americans rejected fats and consumed sugar by the buckets.

Interestingly, even at the time when this deadly blunder was made, it was known that sugar was the enemy. Countless studies proved the dangers of sugar but they were buried under the heavy mount of sugar industry-sponsored scientific articles downplaying the impacts of sugar and beaming the focus on fats.

Brain scans and various studies have shown that sugar is addictive, and the big players in the industry continue to take advantage of this fallout of our brain chemistry.

You will notice a remarkable change in your health if you completely quit sugar of all types- high-fructose corn syrup, sweeteners, table sugar, etc. It goes to show how undeniable the effect of sugar calories are in our body.

Cane juice, maltose, fructose, corn, malt syrup, etc. are all words signifying different types of sugars. Manufacturers try to deceive consumers by not using the word sugar. There are many more of such words and you'll need to know them to be able to identify and stay away from them.

Artificial sweeteners are the enemy. Studies have shown that they lead to an even greater risk of diabetes and can cause cancer.

Sugar alcohols may look like a better alternative, but even they have downsides and if it cannot be avoided, should be kept to a barest minimum. They cause digestive disorders and tamper with your gut. Plus, they're also pretty addictive.

If you must get that sweet taste, use healthier natural alternatives like maple syrup and pure honey.

Our sugar problem is not so much the sugars and sweeteners we add to our food, but the ones manufacturers pre-add to the foods we buy.

It's enough that sugars and sweeteners are highly damaging to human health, but they are no better on environmental health.

When it comes to sugars and sweeteners, there's really no two ways about it. We need to STOP! Gradually, yes, because it is never easy to undo years of habit and addiction, but we can start somewhere.

BEVERAGES
Key Takeaways:

- *Water is the ideal beverage*
- *Green teas are a healthy choice*
- *Sports and energy drinks are recipes for heart attacks*

Ideally, the only beverage we need to drink, and should drink, is water. But that's not the case. Our stores are filled with uncountable drinks, most of which are filled with nasty stuff detrimental to our health. Besides, even water is not so pure these days, thanks to various degrees and kinds of environmental pollution.

We will always need liquids for our survival, but unfortunately, much of the options available today contain way too much sugar, and additives, and preservatives, and pesticide-ridden ingredients... the list is endless.

We know that the ideal is water, pure and unadulterated. Many of us however, still believe orange juice is healthy- no, it's just sugar (except you squeeze organic, whole oranges yourself). So many beverages bearing outrageous claims of 'health' and 'energy' have also been found to be a fountain of lies.

You need to know some things about beverages:

- The evidence stacked against soda and all other sugar-sweetened beverages are overwhelming. Bottomline, they are toxic.

- Coffee is not totally bad for you; it's not totally good either. As much as it is bursting with antioxidants which prevent cancer, it is also a stimulant that stimulates production of harmful hormones. Besides, most of the coffee we drink today are a far cry from the traditional definition and composition of coffee.
- Bottled water is not just potentially bad for your health, it causes damage to the environment. Get a reverse-osmosis water filter if you really want clean water.
- Today's commercially-produced soymilk is a danger that has been linked with inflammation and leaky gut in humans. Try home-made coconut milk or almond milk instead.
- If you must juice, juice vegetables.
- If you must take alcohol, drink wine, and in small quantities. Beers and sugary cocktails should be a no-go area if you care about your health.
- Energy drinks are basically filled with insane amounts of sugar, stimulants, artificial flavorings, and a bunch of other unhealthy additives that are a perfect recipe for heart attacks.
- Green Tea is one beverage you can confidently drink without fearing for your health.

Tea, coffee, and virtually all soda and soft drinks have adverse effect on the environment. If you're going to take tea or coffee or juice, please take the pain to buy only organic.

Water is the ideal, but for the sake of variety, you can take other healthy alternatives like Green Tea, homemade vegetable juices, watermelon water, etc. Stay away totally from Milk, Vitamin waters, Beers, etc.

PART III
WHAT ELSE YOU NEED TO KNOW ABOUT FOOD
Key Takeaways:

- *It is up to you to clean up your plate, and ultimately, your body*
- *If we eat all the right foods in the right quantities, there'll be no need for supplements*

It's all well and good to know the foods to eat and the ones not to, but what about those other important factors that are a part of our nutrition?

There are certain things that should not find their way onto your plates and it's up to you to ensure that. The list is almost endless on such things but a few are

- Processed foods with monosodium glutamate (MSG)
- Processed foods that have been advertised on TV
- Any processed food with ingredients you can't recognize
- Mass-produced plant foods which are usually covered in pesticides and other toxic chemicals. Foods such as celery, grapes, tomatoes, strawberries, and potatoes have a higher risk of pesticide contamination so if you're going to buy them, you should definitely buy organic. Onions, watermelon, and avocados are some of the foods

that have a lower risk of contamination, so you might get away with buying inorganic on those ones.

- Any food with additives such as flavorings and colorings
- Genetically modified products
- Any meat that is not grass-fed or organic

So if there are items that should not be consumed, there are also those that are healthy and can be incorporated into our foods. Some of these are:

- Traditional spices and herbs like turmeric, cinnamon, and cumin.
- Healthy salts, found in foods like carrots and seaweed, and as seasoning, Himalayan pink salt.
- Processed foods with health benefits. Dark chocolate and organic Tofu fall into this category.

The fact that we hardly do any cooking these days has contributed to the increased rates of sicknesses and diseases. We have little to no choice in most of what we eat and eventually, we pump our bodies with mass-produced, harmful substances called food. We need to get back into our kitchens and get cooking, the right way. If we do this optimally, we won't have any needs for nutritional supplements because we'll already be providing our bodies all the nutrients it needs from food. That's not to say supplements are bad, because for most of us in today's fast-paced world, we will need them. If you must take supplements however, be very careful to go with trustworthy brands who produce only the best.

PART IV
THE PEGAN DIET AND HOW TO EAT FOR LIFE
Key Takeaways:

- *Pegan is more of an attitude than a diet;*
- *Thorough cleansing is necessary to rid our bodies of years of unhealthy food damage*

Adopting an ideal diet is one of the best things you can do to enhance your life, but not before cleansing your body from all the damage years of unhealthy eating has caused.

The 10-day programme involves:

- Taking out the trash- sugary foods, toxic foods, processed foods, and foods that cause inflammation
- Stocking up on wholesome foods
- Using the right supplements

Choosing an ideal diet can be a real challenge. There are just too many options nowadays, with advocates of each condemning the others and reiterating why their side is best. Vegan, Vegetarian, Ketogenic, Paleo, Pescatarian... the list is endless. At the end of the day however, they all have their upsides and downsides. The Pegan diet however, is somewhere in between the Paleo and Vegan diets, and basically, this is what it entails:

- Abstaining from sugar in all its forms. It should be eaten rarely and only in small quantities

- A diet consisting mostly of vegetables. Not the starchy kind, but the healthy, organic ones.
- Eating lesser fruits, and most of your fruits should be those with a low glycemic load, like watermelon and berries.
- Abstaining COMPLETEY from genetically modified foods and those tainted with antibiotics, pesticides, and hormones.
- Incorporating healthy fats, such as omega-3 fats in your diet
- Avoiding most nut, seed, and vegetable oils.
- Stay away from dairy if you cannot tolerate it. If you must have it, take only small quantities, and only organic and grass-fed.
- Use meats only as side dishes. They should never be your main food.
- Eat fish that are low in mercy and toxins, like herrings and wild-caught salmon.
- Avoid gluten and its gut-damaging self
- Gluten-free grains are still not the safest, so eat in very little proportions
- Beans should make an appearance in your food only once in a while, and in little quantities.
- Finally, it is important to get tested to determine which foods in the diet will work for you and which will not.

Now, it is easy to think of the Pegan diet as just another one of the lot, but it is more. It is intended as a nutritional model to free you from food fear and bondage and get you feeling your best while living a truly healthy, well-rounded life.

Made in the USA
Lexington, KY
16 June 2018